Tarot

Alex Eagleton

Flighted Pages

FLIGHTED PAGES

PO BOX 981 Gungahlin, ACT, Australia, 2913

First published in Australia 2025

Copyright © 2024 by Alex Eagleton

All rights reserved.

No part of this book may be reproduced in any form or by any electronic or mechanical means, including information storage and retrieval systems, without written permission from the author, except for the use of brief quotations in a book review. No part of this book may be used or reproduced in any manner for the purpose of training artificial intelligence technologies or systems.

A catalogue record of this book is available from the National Library of Australia.

ISBN: Print: 978-0-6458291-1-2 EBook: 978-0-6458291-2-9

To Hang the Masks Upon the Wall

the merry-go-round

To Georgia,

For the never-ending friendship and offering the singular piece of inspiration to write this collection.

Love, A. Eagleton.

Content warning:

This collection contains descriptions of death, abuse, harassment, addiction, and depression.

Part 1

0. The Fool

The bush calls to me.
Its eucalypt trees and wild honey draw me in,
inviting me to know its secrets.
It hides me away in its clearings
where I can float with butterflies and bees,
watch the birds take flight amongst the clouds.

Creativity also calls to me.
Pushing me to express myself in all that I can,
to use my skills and gain new ones.
It calls me to read everyone and everything,
offering soft chairs and warm teas
to accompany my explorations beyond.

Awareness calls me, too.
Magnifying every plant, their petals and roots,
the mushrooms and moss that feed them.
It accentuates all of my beauty,
adoring my body for all it is, for all it does,
when I wake in the morning and when I sleep at night.

Life calls to me.
Urges me to bask in all its glory,

to absorb its peace and happiness into my body.

Like a summer's day at the beach I am left

floating between the seagulls and joyous children,

as easy and simple as that could be.

ALEX EAGLETON

I. The Magician

I sometimes find myself on a pointless venture,
travelling up-creek with neither paddle nor wind.
The boat turns, my thoughts left astray
as the falls rapidly approach, unavoidable now.
At their precipice the question is poised:
"what is art?"

A sociologist might say it is a reflection,
the relationship between the artist and the cosmos manifest –
a bit dull, if you ask me.
A philosopher might say it is expression,
a channelling of all our humanity into a singularity –
also dull, and a bit pompous
(though that might be my bias against philosophers).

What if I reframed it slightly: process or piece?
Is art the process one undergoes in creating
or is it the resulting piece, refined and perfected?
Perhaps it is both;
an expression of our relationship with the universe
refined into a singularity of perfection.

If this is the case, we end with more questions than answers.

Who can create art? How can we create art? Why do we create art?

Maybe this venture isn't so pointless after all.

ALEX EAGLETON

II. The High Priestess

I still remember the first time I had queer sex.

It was unlike anything that had come before,

skin set ablaze beneath awkward fingers and flickering fairy lights.

The first time I had sapphic sex I was swept away in a storm,

butterfly peas and African tulips swirling in the wind.

It didn't have that anxiety and discomfort –

it was intuitive, natural,

and made me redefine every other experience.

A similar thing happened in my first sapphic relationship.

It was the first time I felt someone match me,

truly be my equal in every aspect imaginable.

There was nothing but pure bliss as we cuddled on couches

and lay sleeping in parks, watching the sunset through the leaves.

Sapphics are rumoured to dive in too fast.

But when the feelings are like this,

when the love flows like blood through the veins,

and the sex feels as natural as breathing,

can you blame us?

Wouldn't you chase that with reckless abandon?

I would.

ALEX EAGLETON

III. The Empress

This piece is dedicated to my grandmother, Sue Reichardt. May you rest in peace.

My grandmother's bolognese tastes the same,

even after all these years.

It still tastes like my sister's birthday dinner,

a yearly treat the week after Easter.

It still smells like the log fire she lights in winter

and the small wooden bowls she's had forever.

She taught my mother that recipe

back in the winter of '96.

I was 19 when Mum taught me,

stood in the kitchen under the dogs' hopeful gaze.

A recipe passed down from mother to daughter.

Only, I won't be a mother –

I won't have a daughter to pass this legacy on to,

and yet I don't want it lost from memory.

Certainly, my sister and my cousin might remember,

but I have no say in any of that.

It is a family recipe,

so I suppose I share it with my family,

in our moments of triumph,

huddled together against winter's chill.

Both my grandmother and my mother

made this dish special for me,

flavoured it with herbs and nostalgia,

wine and memories of times gone by.

I hope I can add my own flavours to the mix,

make new memories with the family I choose

and share this legacy with those I love.

IV. The Emperor

Rules are made to be broken. They are made to inhibit the self, to restrict expression and to prevent the loss of control.

Go on, break the rules. See what happens. Express yourself however you want, free from their restraint and desires. Break their rules and make your own, then go and break those too.

Seize back control; release all your inhibitions and unleash yourself upon the world.

Do what you want.

Be who you want.

What's the worst that can happen?

V. The Hierophant

I used to be afraid of visual arts,

how the brushes shook in my hands

and the colours blurred with ambiguity.

Schoolteachers abandoned my artistic education

when I was unable to recreate the sweeping strokes

or understand the emotional complexity of their lessons.

Fifteen years later the brush still shakes,

my eyesight is worse and

the elegant strokes remain a mystery.

I stumble through self-expression,

first using my pen and words and then

by scattering paint haphazardly across the canvas.

I no longer fear artistic traditions and their strict forms

for I learned that tradition needn't be remade or obeyed

if all I want is to express myself.

ALEX EAGLETON

VI. The Lovers

Loving you is an overwhelming experience,

a constant bombardment of emotions

that threaten to devour me whole.

When your featherlight fingertips sizzle on my skin,

exhilaration erupts, burning through my veins.

I find my inhibitions disappear around you

as if each time your lips find mine

ice-cold vodka floods my system.

But when the morning comes,

basked in all its nauseating glory,

I wonder if you were just another mistake.

Loving you is an exercise in self-restraint,

forcing myself to take a breath and resist your depths.

But curiosity conquers any attempt at moderation

fuelling the nascent desire to know all there is,

to explore your personhood as I would the archives;

searching for nothing but knowledge itself in the hope

that I might gain an intimate understanding of you.

And when the dawn filters through high-set windows

exhaustion is incomparable to the joy of knowing you.

I could never have predicted loving you.

Afloat in the liminal space between years

your gravitational field dragged me in and

I was rendered incapable of resisting the pull.

You caught me when I crashed into your arms,

holding me tight as your perfume enveloped me.

Now I fall asleep to your soft touches and

the gentle caress of your voice in my ear

before waking to tangled limbs, whispered breaths

and the knowledge that I am finally home.

ALEX EAGLETON

VII. The Chariot

My therapist said that I need to
"reconfigure my definition of success".

She's right, of course she is,
my current vision is outrageous.

But before I redefine anything
I must ask myself
why two books are not enough,
why an athletic career of ten years is
still a decade too short.

Three languages later and
I am still misunderstood –
by none more than myself.

Perhaps success is between the moments
where joy and hope exist.

Perhaps it is safe friends
and candlelit dinners.

Perhaps success should be vague,

indefinite and disfigured.

Perhaps success shouldn't be measured at all.

I wonder if my therapist would like that.

ALEX EAGLETON

VIII. Strength

There are three of you who stand out against the rest,

three men who have tried their best

to destroy child, teenage, or adult me,

and all of you drowned in Failure's sea.

One of you stole decades from me,

manipulated your abuse so I felt guilty.

I was worn down to a broken child

by malevolent lies and sinister guile.

You were the first I survived.

One of you despised that your daughter loved me.

Harassed and shamed me where all could see.

You destroyed adolescent hopes and dreams,

trapped me in a cage and laughed as I screamed.

You were the second I survived.

The last of you exploited the best of me,

preyed upon the final scraps of hope and naïveté.

You warped our interactions in your favour,

then gorged yourself on my good nature.

You were the third I survived.

I withstood all three of you, your efforts aside.

Endured your exploitation, abuse, and lies.

Each of you hunted, stalked me like prey –

none of you were prepared for when my wrath came.

ALEX EAGLETON

IX. The Hermit

We measure time strangely

in winters endured and summers seen,

in spring births and autumn's close.

Ancient measurements of time

ill-equipped to reflect the truth,

to express the experience of age.

Eventually, we reach a point –

an arbitrary number of

russet leaves crushed and

lambs raised to ewes –

when we are told we are "wise"

as if it were a title to be proud of.

Wisdom is a useful tool,

I'll not deny it that.

But what does it cost when

you're wise beyond your seasons?

A history of pain and

a future of regret?

I think I'd rather be a fool.

X. Wheel of Fortune

The child in the corner still cries occasionally,

though the grip on their pen has loosened

and their scrawled words have grown more legible.

Sometimes I am able to join them for a while,

cross-legged on a cushion in the centre of the room,

our creativity flowing across the page side-by-side.

Or maybe I'll read aloud so they can find some sleep,

cherishing the feeling of their slowing breath in my lap

as I run my fingers through their soft blonde hair.

I take these moments to reflect on the doorway,

remember the times I froze at the threshold,

my own tears falling as I force myself away.

Each time I leave I do so with the knowledge that

tomorrow's decision is still yet to be made

and that the child grows from everything I offer them.

All I can do each time is hope I will have another day.

XI. Justice

Ah, perfection

ever elusive

ever desired.

Ethereal and

incomprehensible.

You float,

tease

every opportunity

never grasped.

Oh, doubt

ever present,

never sought.

Mundane yet

inescapable.

You drag,

claw

at every breath

never released.

XII. The Hanged Man

I refuse to look away,

I dare not even blink.

He walks across the courtyard,

manacles grinding into skin

so blood drips to his feet, pooling

as he stops at the base of the gallows.

He smirks, tosses me a wink

before he is shoved up the stairs.

My eyelids refuse to meet.

The noose wraps around his neck

and he takes a long, slow breath,

savouring the smell of old shit and

his already rotting companions.

The lever is pulled.

He drops.

Just as I hear his neck snap

my eyes slam open,

the space intimately familiar

despite the darkness.

I sigh, roll over, go back to sleep.

ALEX EAGLETON

XIII. Death

This piece is dedicated to Cameron Shelton. May you rest in peace.

Death approached me the week after you two met,

asking if I was certain of the path ahead,

my foot hovering over the flagstones.

I hesitated.

I knew they could see my foot shaking,

see the uncertainly written in every limb.

When they sat me down and embraced me

the warmth of their touch was surprising.

They spoke gently, compassionate of my pain.

They told me of the time you two had spent together,

your unending stubbornness and refusal to leave,

how they had grown fond of you and were sorry to take you.

They seemed resentful of their nature and their role –

though that might be the projection of a mourning soul.

Death comforted me when I turned to them –

in a time of desperation they offered the comfort I needed,

though it was not the comfort I expected.

XIV. Temperance

I often find beauty in the spaces between,

in the times we would otherwise call empty.

The silence that grows in a conversation

the lull of a café after the lunchtime rush

the empty page at a chapter's end

the train ride home at three am

the sheet threads that separate our fingertips.

When we find these moments and stay

grasping them close to our hearts,

we create.

The dash at the end of a line

the gentle strokes in negative space

the final quivers of a semiquaver.

When we live in the spaces between

we find beauty, and we make art.

ALEX EAGLETON

XV. The Devil

It's a strange thing to be placed on a mantle,
to be lifted up and sat beside
those you have long admired without
having taken that step up yourself.
To be treated as an authority,
have people hanging on your every word
before you know what to say.

Don't worry, the discomfort soon abates,
replaced with a pride and hollow arrogance
that desperately fights the voice whispering
"you're not good enough, you don't deserve this."

Those emotions push you further,
drive you down the road faster than you imagine,
making you play catch-up with yourself
as you hurtle towards shiny papers,
medals, trophies, and memorials untold.

But it is all for naught.
You can never catch the doubt
that fuels materialistic ambition.

XVI. The Tower

I drop into the chair by the upstairs window,

crack it open and recoil from the humid breeze.

I set my crystal glass down, brown liquid sloshing,

before pulling a cigarette from the packet.

The lighter's flickering is miniscule against the dark.

I take a sip of my whisky.

Inhale. Exhale.

Tap tap tap against the ashtray.

I look out the window;

the couple next door is arguing.

Their voices reverberate off the light poles,

steadily growing against the pressing darkness.

Something in his tone makes me pause.

I think I want to help, but I don't know how.

I take a sip.

Inhale. Exhale.

Tap tap tap.

I look out the window;

they have become more frenzied,

ALEX EAGLETON

circling each other like snarling wolves

waiting patiently for the time to strike.

She is holding her own in this contest.

I want to help, but I might make it worse.

I take a sip.

Inhale. Exhale.

Tap tap tap.

I look out the window;

I watch them descend through a haze,

my instincts drugged into lethargy and

my brain taking aeons to catch up

to the violence under trembling starlight.

I want to help, but I might be too late.

I take a sip.

Inhale. Exhale.

Tap tap tap.

I look out the window;

he is kneeling on the grass, hands cupping his nose

as rivulets of blood stream through his fingers,

viscous liquid shimmering in the soft moonlight.

A car starts up, backs out, and leaves.

I wanted to help, but I wasn't needed.

I tip the last drops of whisky onto my tongue.

Inhale. Exhale.

I stub out my cigarette in the ashtray.

XVII. The Star

I once wrote of bridges that burned

torched by those who had crossed over.

I once wrote of watching the flames

flicker orange and red and gold.

I didn't write about the dead coals,

the smoke ripped away by a morning gale.

Nor did I write about the chill fog

banked over the ravine, hiding the loss.

I now write about the path out,

down the treacherous mountainside.

I now write about the forest beyond

and a glade where I might find peace.

I will write about the flowers,

their pollen sweet to bees and birds alike.

I will write about solace beneath the trees

one day, I hope.

XVIII. The Moon

Do you get lost in your dreams like I do,

floating through the memories

over your morning coffee,

unable to distinguish the dream from reality?

Or are your dreams fantastical and vivid,

absurdly whimsical in every way,

leaving you snorting crumbs across the table

as you walk back through last night's adventures?

Perhaps you don't remember your dreams,

waking with mind and memory blank,

unimaginable worlds lost to the aether

and your breakfast left undisturbed.

Maybe you dream as you stroll under the sun,

unable to carry on with your day

after wandering through fantasies

that leave you flushed and embarrassed.

Would you share in my dreams with me,

curled under blankets or around a mug,

losing ourselves in the bizarre minutiae,

ALEX EAGLETON

oblivious to the dream we cherish most?

XIX. The Sun

The trees that line the street are out of sync

and beneath their boughs are snapshots of time.

Ochre leaves have abandoned the grey sticks they once called home

and there is a curtain of petals descending from now flowering buds.

Both come to a rest cushioning the footfalls of those who pass.

In between each of the snapped twigs and vibrant leaves

memories and dreams are summoned into the light

bathing that path that leads to that little French café in joy.

ALEX EAGLETON

XX. Judgement

There is something about a perfectly brewed coffee
that makes me feel like I'm in the safest space possible.
It isn't the caffeine addiction, I promise –
it's the care taken in the frothing of milk,
the love in creating a brew for an untold number of people.
That level of care and consideration can't be isolated
but is inevitably transferred to every other aspect of life.

Pair this experience with centuries-old brick walls
decorated in pride and solidarity down every street,
and the most beautiful people I have ever seen,
and I am left feeling unlike I ever have before –
safe and welcomed into a new city by the city itself.

In that moment, as I take the first sip of my second coffee,
a clarity settles, solidifying me in time and space;
this peace, the safety and belonging I feel, is deserved.

I should chase this feeling.
I will chase this feeling.

XXI. The World

A dissonance rings out,

distorting the final beats of the movement,

shattering emotional resonance at the climax.

The final bar eludes me,

harmony breaking rank at every opportunity,

impudent and brazen no matter the accommodation.

Perhaps it's the movement, not the bar.

If individuals cannot work within the system

then it's the system that must change to suit.

I set to revising.

Rewrite the movement and recompose the parts

to tell the story in an unfamiliar way.

As revisions echo through the chamber

the harmony finds space, rising to marvellous completion,

bringing the movement to a close with a flourish.

Part 2

0. The Fool Reversed

Every pawn has dreams buried in their heart –
fantastical visions of becoming something more,
achieving things that are forever out of reach.

I saw an incredible game once
where a pawn was valued beyond belief,
supported and defended by everyone
as its position grew ever stronger.

I wonder what was going through their mind
as they moved up the board.
Did they feel that constant support
from the Queen and her followers?
Did they dare to believe in themselves
as their goal grew ever closer?
I suspect part of them began to crumble,
their buried dreams breaking forth
as desired resolutions seemed inevitable.

I was loathe to be there for the capture,
for the moment the realisation settled on them.
The abandonment dragged them down
as their sacrifice was set in motion,

discarded for the cause – the Greater Good.

All pawns are taught to bury their dreams,
to not trust the system and its architects.
They are, after all, made to be disposed of.

This pawn knew this, was raised in this
and against their better judgement,
against the advice of their peers,
they allowed themselves to dream,
believed they had the right to dream.

ALEX EAGLETON

I. The Magician Reversed

They lean against the front door watching bags slide from their fingers,
not noticing the strange chill in the apartment as exhaustion drags them down,
as it fights to buckle their knees and splay their limbs across floorboards.
With a deep and bracing sigh, they move further into the home,
navigating the liminal space of a pitch-black apartment,
entirely reliant upon muscle memory to drop them onto the bed.

You mumble something unintelligible at the shifting mass on the mattress,
unable to process the garbled response you get as you roll over
stroke your fingers down their spine, press a kiss to their shoulder.

They deflate under the contact, letting tension fall away,
too tired to notice the exhilaration that doesn't shoot through their veins
or the tingles that aren't dancing down their spine at your touch.
They shrug out of their wrinkled and worn clothes with flailing limbs,
stubbornly refusing to stand up from the mattress and ease their own way,
before collapsing into you one final time and kissing you goodnight.

You pray that they don't notice the absent taste of your smile in the kiss,
just as you hope they aren't aware of how your hair falls still
despite the half-conscious devotions they whisper in each languid breath.

II. The High Priestess Reversed

Growing up, I was taught to be terrified of Hell.

I wasn't alone, every Catholic child was taught the same.

We were told the transgressions that would doom us

and that despite prior forgiveness, we could not sin.

I knew that there was something off,

that something inside me didn't align.

The lessons left a bitter taste in my mouth

but I taught myself to swallow it,

unwilling to be damned beyond salvation.

I remember breaking down New Year's Eve of 2015.

High School Musical 2 played in the background

as television networks scrambled to fill the time

between outdated radio hosts and the grand farewell of the year.

When the fireworks echoed across the city,

showering the harbour in rainbow sparks and shimmering light,

an explosion obliterated my ribs, shattered my lungs,

and a horrific realisation took residence in my soul.

A new year and a new truth were greeted that night,

but of the two, I only welcomed one.

ALEX EAGLETON

III. The Empress Reversed

When my fingers slipped, I thought I was lost,
thought the storm would decimate me
and smash what was left against the rocks.
When my hand left hers, I thought it was over,
thought I had let go of my one chance at survival.

Days, weeks, months later I washed up on the shore,
surrounded by countless unknown wrecks
and at the crest of the sand dune was a plaque that read
"*The last remnants of hurricane Alex*".

I glanced around the beach and recognised
the remains of bodies I had once owned
scattered amongst the husks of old relationships.
The fond memories drowned in the storm.

I thought back to the moment I fell,
the last seconds before my hand left hers.
"You're the storm, Alex, you take, and you destroy,
and you will not take or destroy anything more from me."
And with that she let go of me.

The only one who'd offered any stability or direction

had left me to face the storm's wrath alone.

She had let go.

Tears streamed down salt-stained cheeks

as my knees collapsed into the sand beneath me.

She had let go.

I stared at the broken shells of a life I once lived

littered across the pristine shore as the tide rose.

She had let go.

As the tide collected the discarded remains of who I was

I didn't scream or shout or resist.

She had let go.

ALEX EAGLETON

IV. The Emperor Reversed

When the dream came, I was surprised.
It'd been eighteen months since we last spoke –
though I certainly saw you plenty,
tearing me from my dreams
so I could play with the possums and the fruit bats.

This dream was different from the rest.
You were the same as you always were:
unyielding in your judgement and
unforgiving of any transgressions.
There was no need for you to change.
Some of your subjects had lost faith,
but that is the harsh reality of ruling.

No, instead I was the one who had changed.
After all those nights with the fruit bats and possums,
shivering in the branches amongst the gumnuts,
I was the one who finally grew up
to recognise a future without you was possible.

I woke with the kookaburras that morning,
having finally shaken you from my life.
My nights were now free from your terrors,

and my dreams reserved for sweeter loves.

I hear that my betrayal surprised you,

left you fuming night after night after night,

ranting and raving to empty eucalypt leaves

until the dawn eventually swallowed you.

ALEX EAGLETON

V. The Hierophant Reversed

They call us liars,

weavers of falsehoods and deception,

intent on destroying lives and legacies.

They call us dramatic,

overexaggerating our reactions to things

that "just aren't that important."

They call us toxic,

insidiously poisoning their spaces,

dissolving their fraternal bonds.

They call us extremists,

limiting their freedoms and expression,

uncaring of the consequences to others.

We are not liars, these are truths that we tell.

We are not dramatic, only responding as best we can.

We do not dissolve bonds, their power structures do.

We are not extremists, but our wrath will be,

when it comes.

VI. The Lovers Reversed

I sit in the courtyard watching the rain fall,

feeling the water land against hair and skin,

listening to the pitter-patter of drops on corrugated steel,

embellished by the splash of growing puddles.

The fog of my breath, warmed by coffee, fades

as the plants seem to return to life,

every passing minute growing stronger and brighter.

Perhaps the rain will save us too.

I doubt it though;

we are not plants.

ALEX EAGLETON

VII. The Chariot Reversed

Anger swells, raising moored vessels.

Waves build but never crash

as moons wax and wane

and the tides rise and fall.

The autumn equinox brings a king tide

riding higher and deeper

before it enters a rapid retreat,

leaving behind dark sand and grooved shells.

The tsunami surges,

consuming the shore, the bank,

intent on devouring all that's left.

It abates, after a time,

leaving desolation in its wake.

VIII. Strength Reversed

Sometimes the mirror will fail me.

My reflection will stand there and

stare back at me, lost and confused,

as if it doesn't recognise this room,

doesn't know these sheets, these walls, these clothes.

It makes me question it all,

every decision I made,

every step I took down this path –

has it all been a mistake?

Am I doing the wrong thing

and doing it for the wrong reason?

No, this is the correct course,

this is the right path to take.

I am just tired or hungry.

Let's just go to bed.

It will be better tomorrow,

won't it?

IX. The Hermit Reversed

She is quiet in the circle of friends,
watching them talk, quip, laugh,
studying the way they interact,
pinballing off quirked eyebrows
and twitched lips to create a moment
that will become a memory,
that will become a story,
that might one day become a legend –
a core moment in the group's history.

She doesn't need to ponder her role,
the character she portrays in this tale.
She is the forgotten NPC in the adventure,
the broken violin in the orchestra.
But she does get to watch joy flower,
gets to witness these lore-defining moments.
She's grateful for that, at least.

X. The Wheel of Fortune Reversed

Have you ever lost control of yourself,

felt your mind sink into moments of emotion,

rationality slipping through cramping fingers

as you struggle desperately to escape?

Have you ever sobbed uncontrollably,

your ribs shaking loose from your sternum

to fall down your chest cavity

and swim in the acid of your stomach?

How do you manage those moments,

when your agency is dragged through your body

and torn out through your big toe?

How do you cope with the freedom that falls

agonisingly languid like a feather before you,

yet remaining out of reach?

How do you pull yourself from the depths

of swirling and torturous pain,

skin sizzling and bubbling away?

Tell me, I beg of you,

how do I escape this?

ALEX EAGLETON

XI. Justice Reversed

Growing up I loved climbing trees

and even now well into my twenties

it overwhelms me with a childlike glee.

I grew up on stolen Illawarra land

my youth was spent in its branches and waves

mapping night-time paths through its starry maze.

But when I returned after ten years

to sand and earth I thought I knew

the trees I had once loved no longer grew.

"How long had those trees stood?" I wondered

"How long had they watched over this Country,

known its people, its animals, and all their stories?

How much did we lose for an apartment or two?"

XII. The Hanged Man Reversed

The storm looms on the horizon,

darkening the sky,

an impenetrable wall of danger.

The wind is astern,

driving her forwards despite

canvas furled against the mast.

The rudder is stiff,

unmoving, held still

by the grim desires of fate.

Fear will not change the wind,

nor will it loosen the rudder.

So onward she sails towards the storm.

The horizon disappears,

rain lashes skin

and wind howls a thousand cries.

ALEX EAGLETON

XIII. Death Reversed

The yellow petal stands in fierce defiance of nature,

clinging to the daffodil's bud with a suffocating grip

as their siblings rot away, mottled greens and browns

beneath the shadow of their fading yellow insolence.

They refuse to be plucked by the wind,

tossed into swirling leaves and dead flowers

in a final grandiose display of beauty

before joining those already claimed by winter's hand.

Yet for all their resistance, decay still finds them,

eating away at the stem like snails over a tomato

until it collapses beneath its own weight,

discarding the last petal between thin blades of grey,

leaving it to return to the ground once more.

XIV. Temperance Reversed

Each step takes you higher up the marble stairs –

pristine and blindingly white, one step,

then the warm touch of pure gold,

then the sparkling ocean under noonday sun,

then the shimmering of blood just spilled –

before they return to pristine cleanliness, and repeat.

You don't notice this, though.

The shining light at the top of the stairs

draws you in, gentle and encouraging,

consuming every fleeting thought in your mind.

The sky flickers behind the light,

pastel pinks and sunset oranges melt into

midnight blues and glowing volcanic reds.

You don't notice this either.

As you approach the light a silhouette forms,

and this time you do notice how the edges blur,

how wings and horns shift in and out of view.

It speaks in your mind, image stuttering with every word:

"Come, my child, you have been chosen."

ALEX EAGLETON

It wants you, and you do not care how or why.

Desperate to be liked and terrified of being hated,

you obey without question, climbing higher.

You come close enough to notice details,

arched eyebrows over molten eyes,

a gentle smile beneath a button nose,

horns smoothly curling from the brow

and cheekbones you could cut yourself on.

A divine allure and a hellish desire rise,

pulling you forward on mindless footfalls.

It beckons you, silent now, and you follow willingly,

charmed at the idea that this indescribable being

has chosen you above all others,

that you might finally be wanted.

You don't notice the flickering of the sky slow,

how the midnight blues fade into flaming yellow and red.

You don't notice the horns stay nor molten eyes

watching you with unblinking intensity.

You don't notice how you fall

the moment your fingers touch theirs.

XV. The Devil Reversed

Have you ever witnessed someone have their main character moment,

seen someone grasp that call with both hands

so tight that you worry it'll shatter in their face?

If you ever have the honour of witnessing that occurrence,

pay attention to their eyes, wide and eager,

absorbing anything and everything from their bearded mentor.

Watch the way they gleam at any opportunity to prove

they are everything they've been told they're not,

at the chance to finally own their agency.

I saw this on the train last week, on my way home from the city.

It didn't take long for me to know what I was seeing.

I've never seen that person before, and I may never see them again.

But I hope that they can defeat their Big Bad

and find a space for themselves to live, and to be happy.

ALEX EAGLETON

XVI. The Tower Reversed

When the future shared itself with me I collapsed,

the weight of its potential crashed into me

and pulled me down into the darkness,

into the depths of possibility and avoidance.

There are ways to avoid what seems inevitable,

a part of me desired and adored them from afar,

paths that shine brighter than a legion of angels.

And yet, there was a part of me that hesitated.

And in that moment, the smallest of voices spoke,

daring to whisper against the raging storm that pulled me down:

"What if?"

What if we embraced the future however it came?

What if we strived forwards without fear?

What if we chase our passions farther than imaginable?

What if we didn't let doubt control our decisions?

What if we wanted to experience more, to live our best life?

What if we wanted to love ourselves and, bear with me on this,

what if we let ourselves be happy?

XVII. The Star Reversed

Teetering on the brink of adulthood

they follow, believing blindly,

critical thought set aside

for it brought only discomfort

and hatred of the self.

The perfect circus monkey,

willing to ignore all that was wrong

for the chance at a delicious treat.

When that monkey fell off the edge

into the broad and overwhelming world,

treats were no longer offered

and work was taken for granted.

No longer bribed into a false security

the monkey went on a search,

dug through cupboards of the past

in hope of finding those forgotten skills.

When they were found in the depths

rust had almost entirely devoured them.

So the monkey worked to restore them,

treating them like antique tools

until they were ready to be used again.

ALEX EAGLETON

The monkey left that year,

setting off to correct their mistakes,

repair what had been torn from them

and what they had torn from others.

XVIII. The Moon Reversed

It looks like I was wrong –
I apologise for that.
I allowed myself to get swept up
in the emotions and the fantasies;
you know how we poets are,
always the romantics.

The situation isn't what I thought;
I misread those lines,
misinterpreted those edits,
completely missed the director's notes.

It happens, I'm afraid.
Life is rarely so simplistic,
and neither are the relationships we build.
We do not live in a romance novel
and for a moment I forgot that.

Once again, I am sorry, *mon cœur*.
I should treat you better,
should act with more restraint and
with greater care for my actions.
I'll be better next time, for us,

ALEX EAGLETON

I promise.

XIX. The Sun Reversed

I watch the bags grow heavier
on the other side of the screen.
The brightest blue eyes I know
have grown dull and lifeless.
The forehead strains against it all,
trying to keep the eyebrows afloat.

Her hair is clean despite it all,
shining with new wax and oils.
Fingernails are cut into fine curves,
filled smooth and tidy.
Nonetheless, I can feel her clawing at the dirt,
trying to haul herself up the mountainside.

I wish there was more I could do;
throw a rope, carry her up the mountain –
I could be the Samwise to her Frodo!
Alas, there's nothing more to do.

All I can offer are my kindest words
wrapped in my softest tones,
delivered in the depths of friendship.
Be as gentle and supportive as I can

ALEX EAGLETON

through the glass screen in my hand

as the moon sets and the possums sleep.

Another night has passed us by,

another survival, another existence,

as the sun rises once more.

XX. Judgement Reversed

The first time I ordered a coffee I was terrified.
Just a fifteen-year-old kid staring at a chalkboard,
countless options before me but none of the knowledge.
I didn't know what I liked, which roasts or milks were best –
I was fifteen years old and barely knew my own name.

Three years later I walked into Dan's and stared once more,
instantly overwhelmed by the sheer volume of decisions.
At eighteen I knew my name, how I liked my coffee,
and how to cite the bible in Chicago, Harvard, and MLA.
I couldn't imagine knowing what alcohol I liked.

By the time I was twenty-one I loved both coffee and alcohol
but had lost who I was as I raced from who I might become.
I didn't know what addiction looked like on me,
didn't realise how it clung to my shoulders like a wet coat,
warding off emotions as if they were a winter storm.

My coffee order and favourite cocktail changed over time
as my palate evolved and my social circles shifted.
And over the course of a few tumultuous years
I ignored the risks in the comfort they brought me,
reliable and continuous in a period of constant change.

ALEX EAGLETON

But I did eventually learn that there were consequences,

that the choices I made had repercussions beyond myself.

Coffee and alcohol were not my only addictions,

but at twenty-four, coffee is the only one I still partake of

and I have found peace with who I am, at last.

XXI. The World Reversed

All things end.

We are told that endings matter,
that they make the life we live worthwhile,
the love we share sweeter.

And so too must this collection end.
The ink has run dry in my pen,
the pages have stopped turning.
This tale has been told.
Its questions have been asked
and its lessons learned.

I suppose my story will end one day;
the sagas I share and the movements I make
will reach their final notes, their last positions.

However, I intend to keep writing.
If you plan to keep reading,
then maybe it will never end.

Would that make it any less sweet,
any less worthwhile?

Acknowledgements

First, I would like to acknowledge the traditional custodians of the land on which this collection was created, the Ngunnawal and Ngambri peoples. I pay my respect to their elders, past and present, as well as all their artists and storytellers who have created here too. I acknowledge that I live and work on stolen Aboriginal land, and that sovereignty was never ceded.

Secondly, I would like to thank Georgia for giving me the inspiration to write this book. All it took was one comment on an Instagram post from early 2023 and you set me on this path. You've always encouraged and supported my creativity and I feel blessed to count you amongst my closest friends.

To all my those around me who provided feedback on drafts, early and late, I cannot say how much I appreciate you. Maia, Sara, Lawren, and Merri, you are incredible artists and even better friends. Thank you. Of course, these are not the only friends who have supported me throughout the creation of this collection. There are countless others who have listened to half-baked lines or endured an impromptu reading, and to all of them I will be forever grateful.

To my editor, Tricia Dearborn, it has been a pleasure to work with you again. Thank you for all your insight and expertise, the collection would not be the same without you.

Sara, you have completely outdone yourself with this cover art. You are an inspiration across all mediums and working with you is one of the greatest honours in my life. I do not think that words can properly express how much our friendship means to me.

Finally, to you, the reader. If you have read each piece between these covers or only skimmed a couple lines, I am grateful for your time nonetheless. I am astounded that there are so many who wish to hear what I have to say. Conceptualising it is incredibly difficult and I will always be grateful for this opportunity.

Much Love,

A. Eagleton xx

TAROT

P.S. A final thank you to all the cats who suffered during the creative process more than any of my friends. Kit, Swoop, Yuki, and Vincent I love you all so much. Thank you for your intelligent and honest feedback.

About the Author

Alex Eagleton is a queer author and poet writing on Ngunnawal and Ngambri land. Her debut collection *To Hang the Masks Upon the Wall* was released in 2023, with a second collection released later that year. When not juggling too many projects at once, Alex can be found reading, studying, or playing TTRPGs, all whilst drinking too much coffee.

You can find Alex on any of the following social platforms:

instagram.com/eaglespoet

tiktok.com/eaglespoet

twitter.com/eaglespoet

www.ingramcontent.com/pod-product-compliance
Lightning Source LLC
Chambersburg PA
CBHW031301290426
44109CB00012B/680